Shaped By God

Aquanetta,
May God continue to
keep you while shaping
you in his hands.
Love,
Evangelist Velma Nelson-Griffin

Velma R. Nelson

DEDICATION PAGE

I would like to take this opportunity to dedicate this book in loving memory of my grandparents;

Rev. Francis C. Rose Sr., Lucinda Waites Rose, and Johnnie Johnson Giddens and to my aunt Faye. I would also like to dedicate this book to my parents; Bennie and Gladys Nelson, a dear friend of mine, Jeanette Washington, and to my siblings whom I love dearly.

Rev. Francis C. Rose Sr., my grandfather, was a real warrior. I can still visualize my grandfather sitting in the pulpit with his legs crossed wearing his white suit and burgundy and white shoes. On other occasions, I can picture him standing behind the pulpit singing "Precious Lord." At that time in my life I didn't know how precious the Lord really was. I remember the days that I would go visit him just to be able to sit and listen to his words of wisdom. He inspired me in a lot of ways.

My maternal grandmother, Lucinda Waites Rose, whom I came to know later in my adult life, was a soft spoken woman. I can still hear her saying "foot" and "I'm alright." Those were her phrases, but I knew what she meant.

My paternal grandmother, Johnnie Johnson Giddens, whom I miss dearly, was a jewel to me. Growing up, she was my angel. She provided me with the things I desired and the things she desired for me to have. She was a great dominos player and taught my brothers and me how to play. At other times she was working in her flower beds. She seem to have so much joy in doing that, that I became inspired to grow flowers because of the joy I saw in her while working in her flower gardens.

To my beloved aunt, Nettie Mae Walker, who was a fighter. She endured much through her failing health but she never allowed that to stop her from praising God anyhow. Watching her reminds me of the scripture, **(Psalm 34: 1); "I will bless the Lord at all times: his praise shall continually be in my mouth."** By watching her preserver and seeing the things that was taking place in her life makes me want to keep on keeping on until God says it's enough.

To my dear parents, Bennie Joe and Gladys Nelson, who are the best parents on this side of Heaven. Words can not express the love and sacrifice they express towards me. To them I am the baby eagle that has learned to spread her wings and soar to the highest heights that God has for me. My mother often says to me when I am down, **"And we know that all things work together for the good of those who love the Lord and are called according to his purpose" (ROMANS 8:28).** I thank God for each of you.

To my dear friend, Jeanette Washington, who kept nagging me to complete this book. Every time I talked to her on the phone, she asks me about it. She always said, "God gave you that and you need to finish the book." Well, Nett, it's done. Love you girl.

To my sisters and brothers who are truly a blessing to me. I thank each of you for the treasures that we shared together. As we all became adults and went our separate ways, we kept that love connection among us. Distance did not and cannot separate our love, for we have a saying, "One for all and all for one." I love you guys forever. Thank each of you for putting up with me.

Because of who God is in my family's lives, is the reason that I am who I am in God today. They taught me that it is because of God's grace and mercy that I can stand and declare victory in the Lord for his word says, **"Know ye that the Lord he is God: it is he that hath made us, and not we ourselves; we are his people, and the sheep of his pasture" (Psalm 100; 3).**

In reading this book you should become inspired in knowing that God is God and will do just what he said he would do. Trials may come, storms may rage, but know that God is still in control. God is a good God all the time and all the time he's good.

The cover of my book describes my life.

The black represents me being in total darkness.

The purple letters mean God brought me out of the darkness into the light of royalty meaning I have part ownership of all that belongs to God.

The letters being in 3-D represents the struggles of life I had to go through in order to write this book.

The clay pot with cracks and my picture fading into it means I've been broken into pieces.

The hands holding the pot represents God still have his hands on me.

CONTENTS

INTRODUCTION PAGE

This book is an inspiration to all who endure the heart ache and pains of everyday living. It tells a story of how God shaped me in my spiritual, financial, emotional, and physical life. Many times in my life, I thought I was down for the count but God said no. Living life has taught me that things are not always as they appear and that we must live our life according to the word of God. We must all have a vision, for the word of God says, **"Where there is no vision, the people perish: but he that keepeth the law, happy is he" (Proverbs 29; 18).**

As you read this book, my prayer is that the spirit of God will touch your heart and you too will realize that God can and will do the same for you.

Many of us have thorns that we may never overcome but we must keep our focus and know that God is still God. He has a plan for your life as well as mine. This I know because he said so in his word; **"For I know the plans I have for you," declares the Lord, "plans to prosper you and not to harm you, plans to give you hope and a future." (Jeremiah 29:11).**

Lift your head up and know that God has your back.

CHAPTER 1

CHILDHOOD DAYS

Oh mighty God, mighty God, thank you for blessing me. A country girl; born in a small country town on a hot summer day in late August in the year of 1963, with a purpose. I had a many challenging days ahead.

Before my mother gave birth to me, God already had a purpose for my life. Born into a family with five other siblings, my mother taught us the value of being a family. You would just have to know my mother. She is a kind Godly woman who is always putting everyone else's feelings, hopes, and dreams before her own. She worked many long hard hours but always found the time to plan for family outings.

I remember one particular outing that we took to Six Flags in Dallas, Texas. My parents had packed lunches and drinks and loaded it and us into my papa's pick-up truck bed with a camper on top. We were so excited about going that it didn't matter that it was hot in the back of the truck. We song many songs, played "I spy something," and enjoyed each other's company.

My mother instilled within each of us the importance of family and taught us how to stand together in bad times as well as the good times. Because of this lesson, we became loving individuals that grew to love the Lord and mankind.

During the summer months we all had chores. While our classmates were hanging out in the neighborhood, we had to stay home. We could not go to other neighborhood children houses because my mother said there were too many of us and we had to learn how to play with each other while learning responsibility. At this precious time in my life, God was already beginning a mighty work in me by teaching me the lesson of loving my sisters and brothers and how to get along with family. Later in life I would learn just how important family really was and that family extended far beyond household members.

My parents both worked, so; my older brother was placed in charge of us, making sure that we completed our chores while at the same time making sure we stayed out of trouble. Being rebellious, I never wanted to do what I was told by my older brother, Joe. He often tried to enforce what mama told each of us to do and it caused many fights among us. Many times my father was called home from work to discipline me. As we grew into mature adults, I grew to love and respect Joe in many ways as well as other people in authority regardless of their age.

My oldest sister, Marilyn, was one of God's special children who has a learning disability and sometimes used her disability as a crutch. She acted like she couldn't do certain things and I in turn had to do them. We fought because of this. I didn't understand at that time in my life that God has a purpose for each of us and that sometimes it meant being different. At this early age in life, God was beginning to shape me by teaching me how to treat people that are different. Later in life I would discover why God was preparing me for such a task. As we grew up I learned to love her unconditionally and to accept the things she couldn't do and thank God that he had placed me in her path to help her in all the ways I could.

When there were no chores to do we all played together and many talents were discovered among us. We learned how to shoot basketball, taught by my second oldest brother, Joe Nathan. (Just in case you haven't figured it out, yes, there are two brothers named Joe. Such a unique family I have). He was good in sports and participated in many school athletic activities.

Joe and I are the middle children and there is a special bond between us. Many years later we would discover just how bonded we really are.

At other times we were taught by our father about horses. My father is a real cowboy and taught us how to ride horses with or without a saddle. My father is a wonderful man with a kind spirit. He was also known as the black cowboy of our town. He taught us how to run up behind horses and jump upon their backs like Indians did on T.V. If you need to know anything about a horse, just ask my dad.

There were other times I wanted to play with my baby sista, Andrea. She and I were not close growing up because of the age gap between us. I remember dragging her out of bed when she was an infant, just because I wanted to hold her. As we grew to become adult women we became best of friends and shared many things. I had no idea at this time in my life, but even though she was younger, she would become my shoulder to lean on.

As we all grew up we learned how to appreciate the little things in life. Back in those days, I like to call them the good ole' days, there were no competition as to who had what because everybody had the same thing, **Family.**

Because we lived in a family block we always had something to do. My great uncle lived behind us, my great aunt on the opposite side through our back yard and my grandmother lived on the side of her.

16

At my great uncles house were many old cars to tinkle with and goats to play with. We sometimes hung out there if there was nothing else to do. He wasn't too friendly but we knew he loved us in his own way.

Our great aunt's house was a little more exciting. She had all kinds of fruit trees to eat off of. I had no idea at this time in my life but God was at work shaping me, for later in life I was to learn that the fruit of the spirit would be my road map to eternity. Seeing all the fruit to eat was just giving me a glimpse of what was to be. My aunt had many chickens for us to play with. At first I was afraid of them but after many visits, I got use to them. She taught my baby brother, David, and I how to feed the chickens and remove eggs from under the hens. That's when I realized that only hens laid eggs, not roosters.

My brother and I liked dealing with the chickens and looked forward to visiting my aunt's house. Because we fought each other and were so mischievous when we were linked together, my aunt and grandmother would only keep us separately. As we grew older he became my protector. He was always there to fight my fights that I often started with other children.

Our aunt figured she could keep us occupied and out of trouble by giving each of us a little biddy (baby chick) that we named Jack and Jill. Jack, a little black biddy, was my brother's, and Jill, a little yellow biddy was mine. My aunt Luella built a cage for our baby chicks but the cage was not too sturdy and a neighborhood dog got into the cage and ate our pets. We cried for many days. God was at work once again by teaching me that nothing last forever and through this walk of life there will be much heartache.

At my grandmothers house was a tire swing and many trees to climb. She had many beautiful rose bushes and taught me how to cut the roses off the bush without getting caught by the thorns. Again I didn't realize it, but God was shaping me by teaching me that in this life, I would encounter many thorns. Some were to be removed and some would not.

As I continued to grow in age, my focus began to change. I no longer wanted to cause my sisters and brothers heartaches. They sure were glad. By now they had many bruises left by me and had begun to dislike me.

I became interested in boys. I was very disobedient and became pregnant at the age of 14. I gave birth to a son just before my 15th birthday. Many said,

"I wouldn't amount to anything and I wouldn't graduate, that I had thrown my life away," but God had another plan for me. Because of my disobedience, I had delayed the process of where God was taking me but I had not stopped it, for whatever God has ordained for me to do, will be done. God was using what man saw as a bad thing for his good.

Later in life I was to learn that God orders my steps for he allowed me to know through his word, **"And we know that all things work together for the good to them that love God, to them who are the called according to his purpose" (Romans 8:28).**

I would later learn that nothing just happens and God allows things to happen in our every day life to keep us from something more harmful and/or to keep us on the road to spiritual growth. I had no idea how my life would turn out but God did. He began to shape me through the choices and situations that I had placed myself in.

CHAPTER 2

LIFE AS A YOUNG MOTHER AND WIFE

My days ahead were very challenging. I spent many sleepless nights up with my baby but I continued to press on by attending high school. I had a strong determination to be somebody extraordinary someday. God had placed a seed within me that he was cultivating through trials and tribulations in my life. I didn't understand a lot that was taking place in my life, but God knew. He was at work shaping and molding me by teaching me perseverance and preparing me for what I was to later become. God built a fire deep within me that gave me a burning desire to press on against all odds.

At the age of 16, I married Julius. I didn't know at this time in my life to ask God for a mate. I would later learn that ignorance is very costly. As a young mother and wife, I really thought I had it going on. I had money to spend and plenty of sex. Needless to say, I really didn't have a clue to what life was all about. After the newness of being a mother and a wife wore off (in other words, the veil removed from my eyes), I saw it was not all I thought it to be. Between going to school full-time, being a mother, wife, and working a part-time job, everything begun to take a toll on me. There were times I wanted to give up but I had a praying mother that helped out as much as she could and encouraged me not to give up, to seek God and attend regular church services.

Ignoring my mother's advice about attending church services on a regular basis, I continued doing my daily activities, thinking I could fix all the problems that I encountered. It seemed that every time I turned around something else was occurring. I began to realize and recognize that God was my source. After finishing high school, my burdens became a little lighter. Julius was blessed with a job making a good salary so he decided that I could be a stay at home mom. I was about to learn a valuable lesson. I was now totally dependent upon Julius (which is what I was suppose to do) to take care of me and our child. Things changed drastically. Because I had no income coming into the household, Julius begin to act as if I didn't matter and that I should accept whatever he dished out to me. Sometimes he would leave the house and I would see him the next day. He only paid bills if I did just as I was told, otherwise, he would take his check and spend it on whatever he chose.

I remember one particular incident when Julius had gotten paid, bills were due, food was needed, and we had gotten into an argument. The argument escaladed into a physical altercation, leaving me with a busted lip and him leaving the house along with his paycheck while my child and I were left with no food or money to buy food. He showed up the next day as if nothing had taken place. This was becoming the norm.

Many nights I wondered if there would be lights the next day or food in the house to eat. Life became a chore to overcome and not a joy to live.

I developed many bumps and bruises. I began to think this was the norm for being married. To make matters worse I became pregnant with our 2nd child. After numerous fights we separated and I became a welfare recipient.

Julius had no interest in helping support our child. He was too busy living his own life. I remember Christmas was approaching and I had stretched my welfare check as far as I could, so I asked Julius to get our son a few toys. He said he would but he never came through. To make matters worse, the only television set that was in the house was repossessed because I couldn't afford to make the payments on it. I didn't understand how someone could be so heartless.

I was beginning to become depressed. I had no friends to call upon because I had severed all those ties once I got married. Julius had convinced me not to hang out with old friends because I was married and they weren't. He thought they would be a bad influence on me. Later in life, I would learn that his goal was to keep me isolated from the world so I would not realize that marriage was not about him controlling me.

My family was very supportive of me and helped out as much as they could. Once again my mother began to probe me about attending regular church services. Because of her persistent prayers and encouragement, I began to attend Sunday morning services. I enjoyed the singing but I hated when it came time for the preacher to speak. I thought "this was so boring," and I soon quit going. I would later learn that what the preacher was speaking about was the word of God, which was the meat of the service and that is what I needed to survive in this world.

During the next several months, I began to really look at my life and I was not happy by what I saw. I was not content being on welfare and did not want to be another statistic of society. I did not have time to be a mother to my child because of my fears of how I would survive and how I would provide food and clothing for my baby. Yes, my family was there, but I knew it was not my family's responsibility to take care of me and my child, besides; I was too embarrassed to allow my family to know the pit I was in.

Later in life, I would learn that it was not about what I wanted, but what God wanted for me. God was at work shaping me by allowing me to experience being powerless over my situation so that I would learn how to become totally dependant upon him. He let me know that the situation may be a dead situation but he ain't dead. God was showing me that he is in control of all and he can resurrect anything and anybody, in their dead end circumstances.

After giving birth to a baby girl, I became employed at the town's nursing home and Julius and I reconciled.

Once again I thought things were beginning to work out for the better. How wrong I was. Because of Julius's arrogance, he lost his job. The pressures of my home life became overbearing and I became much stressed.

I cried each morning before going to work because I hated my job so much. It seemed that the more I strived to do better, the worse things got. Julius refused to keep the baby and I had to pay a baby sitter. He said she was too little and he could not stand to take care of her. I thought to myself, "here we are with not enough money to pay our bills, he's not working, and he ain't trying to help with the expenses at all." Not only was I stressed, but I was **angry**. I began to see him in a different light. I resented him for the lifestyle that my children and I had to endure.

He continued doing what he had always done, and acting as if it didn't matter. I began to seek God through prayers. Later in life, I would learn that God was pruning me by allowing me to go through something's.

Six months after reconciliation with Julius, I became pregnant with our third child. I thought my world had come to an end. I began to question God. I didn't understand how this could be happening to me, especially since I was on a birth control pill. I said to God, **"WHY ME O GOD, I ALREADY HAVE TWO CHILDREN, WHAT AM I SUPPOSE TO DO WITH A THIRD?"** I didn't know it then, but that third child was who God was going to use to turn my life around.

You see, God took the pregnancy of that third child to show me his miraculous power.

My mother continually probed me about attending regular services and seeking God for his will for my life. Once again, I began to attend worship services but I was going for the wrong reasons. I thought that by being in church God wouldn't allow bad things to take place in my life. Later in life, I was to learn that you can't fool God anytime. God was teaching me that it rains on the just, just as it rains on the unjust. This time I had decided that I was going to stay within the house of fire and learn about God. I was tired of getting a taste of God by attending services every now and then.

I continued to attend worship services and my focus on life began to change. At this point I was beginning to know God but I still didn't have a personal relationship with him. I began to have a burning desire to know more and learn more about God. I was about to learn that no pain, no gain. God was teaching me that he doesn't impose the pain but he sometimes allows me to go through it so that I will develop fundamental skills needed to survive.

I began to have self-esteem and desire more for myself and my children. I wanted them to enjoy some of the same things that other children did without having to rely upon my parents. I decided to sit Julius down and talk with him about the present conditions of our lives. He decided that he wanted his family and he would step up to the plate and be the provider. Soon after that Julius was able to land another job.

I thought things were getting better. Again, how wrong I was. I lost my job, was six months pregnant and we had no insurance. I thought I would die. I threw my hands up but this time not to give up but for help from God. I didn't know what I was going to do but I knew who to call out to.

Later in life, I would realize that God was working in my life by taking the job I hated so bad and replacing it with a blessing that he had for me.

I went to the employment office to sign up for my unemployment and discovered that there was an opening in the kitchen of a hospital some 26 miles away from my home town. I put an application in and was later called for an interview. During my conversation over the phone with the lady, I revealed to her that I was six months pregnant. She told me that I was the most qualified applicant but I would have to wait until after the baby was born before I could start. I became down about not receiving the job but this time I began to pray.

Within an hour, the lady called back. She said that she had talked to her boss and I could go ahead and start employment. I was beginning to see God's grace and mercy alive in my life. I began to praise God and thank him.

I had to attend orientation classes before beginning my duties. I found out that I would be eligible for health insurance right away and that vacation and sick leave would occur each payday. I was so thankful for the blessings that God was placing upon my life.

Before the birth of my third child, God began to show me favor. My co-workers loved me and I them. I enjoyed my job and came to know many of the employees within the hospital. By the time delivery day came, I was well known. Later in life, I would learn that God was preparing me for what he had in store for me by giving me people skills and allowing me to have a great impact upon the lives of the people I came in contact with.

So much love was shown towards me and I was given many gifts for my baby. Oh how I thanked God. God had taken me from a job that I hated with no insurance and not knowing how I was going to pay the expenses for a new baby to a job with medical insurance that paid all but $100.00 of my medical expenses. I was beginning to recognize the power of God, as well as his favor.

Over the next several months, my baby became sick and stayed that way for some time so I was forced to quit my job and stay home with her. I would later learn that every thing is but a season, for God says in his word, **"To everything there is a season, and a time to every purpose under the heaven" (Ecclesiastes 3:1).**

I realized that God had placed that job in my life for that time to supply what I needed for that time.

My children and I continued attending church services and I became the best wife and mother that I knew to be. After many months, my children and I began to attend mid-week services. I began to feel like God had more for me to do and I had developed a hunger for the word of God.

One Wednesday night sitting in bible study, God poured out the Holy Spirit all over me. I knew without a shadow of a doubt that I was saved. I recognized God for who he was; my savior. That summer all three of my children were baptized. Oh, how I thanked God.

I felt my life was on track with God but there were other issues coming about. I didn't have a job and money was scarce. Since I had developed self-esteem, I didn't want just any job. God had placed something greater within me. I wanted to have a career so I enrolled in college. I encountered much opposition from Julius. I didn't understand why he would not want me to better myself. After all, it was for the benefit of the family. Again God was shaping me by teaching me how to overcome the negative things that were apart of my life. I was learning that if God be for you, he is more than the world against you. I became determined to be somebody against all odds.

I later graduated from college with an associate degree and God blessed me with a job making more than I thought I ever would. As I began to settle into a comfortable lifestyle, I began to have an uneasy feeling. I didn't understand why, since things were somewhat better. I was to later learn that this uneasy feeling was God moving in my life, preparing me for what was to come.

CHAPTER 3

COMING TO KNOW GOD

After working on my job for several months, it was no longer satisfying to me. I thanked God for the job but felt as if he had something else for me to do. I wanted more than just a decent paying job; I wanted a career, so I decided to go to airline school. I had caught on to who I was and whose I was so settling was not in the plan anymore.

To complete my training for airline school, I had to fly to Tampa, Florida. Julius didn't like the idea of me going out of state but I was determined to make a better life for myself as well as my children so I pressed on.

This was such a new and rewarding experience for me. It was the first time I had ever flown and the first time I had ever been away from my home town and family but it was so exciting. I didn't know it then but God was preparing me by allowing me to experience solitude, for later in life I would have to adapt to be alone, just him and me.

While in Florida, I met many friends. One would turn out to be a lifetime friend. God had placed her there for me. God was at work once again, placing people in my life that would be a help to where he was leading me. He was setting me up for the path that he had designed for my life.

After graduating from airline school, I was blessed with a job with an airline in a city some 26 miles away. My job was fun and challenging. I had a joy deep down inside that even I couldn't understand at times.

By now the devil was beginning to grow a little weary of me because I was no longer doing what wasn't pleasing to God. I had begun to seek God for answers and rely upon his guidance. The devil knew that he better get his plan in order or he was about to lose this one. He began to use Julius to work on me.

Julius became jealous of my accomplishments and tried to make life for me unbearable so I would have to quit my job. He stopped helping with the children and began to live his life as a carefree adult with no responsibilities. My mother stepped in and began to help me with the children. Thank God for my mother. Trusting God, I continued to press on. Julius saw that his not being there was not hindering me being able to work so he began to take other avenues. I knew the devil was just using him as a tool to try to stop me from doing the work of the Lord, so I kept moving forward. My focus was on God and what he wanted me to do. I couldn't understand how Julius could act and feel like he did because I was trying to encourage him to go to church, along with the kids and me. He veered in the opposite direction. The pressures of home life were tough but still I trusted God to work it out. I thank God that he kept me through all the heartaches and pains that I was experiencing in my life.

As I continued to attend services, different doors within the church began to open. There were many doors that would later become known to me as the foundation of where God was leading me. I was asked to teach a bible class for the little children. I thought to my self, "There is no way I can do that, I don't know much myself." I didn't know it then but God was setting me up to study and become deeper involved in his word. I was placed over a bible class where I began to teach the little children about the word of God. As I was teaching them, I was learning along with them. God was at work shaping me by teaching me to study to show thyself approved. I became so wrapped up in teaching and the activities within the church that I forgot about all the issues that were taking place in my personal life. The things that had once dominated me didn't seem so important anymore. I began to realize that God had a mighty work for me.

I began to experience the joy that only God can give. I felt like I was on top of the world. My children were learning about God, I was learning about God, and I thought I was on the road to success because I had the idea job. God was about to teach me a lesson by showing me that things are not always as they appear and success does not come from the things that I acquire on earth but from what I acquire for eternity with him. He was using this job as a stepping stone to where he was leading me. God knew that because **I thought** I had the idea job, that when the time came for me to move on, it would be difficult, so he allowed unpleasant situations to occur in the workplace. My supervisor began to lie on me and make the work environment very uncomfortable. Still trying to hold onto what I wanted, I pressed on. Soon after my mother began working overtime and I had no one to watch my children. I was forced to make a decision, to take another shift with different days off so that I could be at home with my children. This made a difference in me being able to attend church services. Later in life I would learn that God sometimes allow unpleasant situations to occur in order to move us from a negative environment into a positive one.

Once again I began to cry out to the Lord for his guidance. I knew I had to have a job because of the present conditions that my life was in. I asked God to send me a job where I could be with my children and attend worship services. God did just that. He blessed me with a job at the local hospital working Monday thru Friday and off on weekends.

That next year of my life was quite an experience. I experienced many valley experiences. I would later learn that the valley experiences came to shape and mold me into what God had me to become, to teach me how to stand when the burdens got so heavy. It would be the valley experiences that would teach me how to manage the problem instead of the problem managing me. It would be the valley experiences that taught me tough times don't last but tough people do.

After a year of working at the hospital, I began to feel dissatisfied. Later in life I would learn that the dissatisfaction was God moving me closer to my purpose. After praying for a revelation from God, I applied for a job at a high school in a city about 15 miles away and was given the job. I was the only black on the teaching staff but I felt so loved. God was teaching me that being different was not a bad thing but an advantage (a lesson that I would have to fall back on later in life).

As I began my duties of working with the children, I began to reach out to them, helping them in every area of their lives that I could. The children didn't know how to receive love and responded back by doing hurtful things to me. Things that sometimes made me cry. Again God was shaping me by teaching me to love in spite of, a lesson that was just in a nick of time for what was about to take place next in my life. You see, God never sends a storm to you without preparing you for it.

Financial burdens within my household began to soar and I decided to take a second job through the school system's janitorial department. The work was physically harder than what I was use to and the supervisor was ungodly. Now I knew why God had taught me the lesson of loving in spite of. I also realized that sometimes you got to do jobs you don't want to do to survive, so I continued working and praying. After the school year ended, I was placed in a bank cleaning after hours instead of the schools. I was beginning to grow a little tired and weary because of the second job but I continued to press on. God was shaping me by teaching me to pray without ceasing and to be satisfied with the job that he had given to me at this time. I began to go to work praising God, singing, and praying.

One day as I was vacuuming, I began to pray and ask God to send me a job making the amount that would total both jobs that I was working. I was reminded of God's word, **"Ask, and it shall be given you; seek, and ye shall find; knock, and it shall be opened unto you"** **(MATTHEW 7:7).**

God began to minister to my spirit and said to me, "Go to ASA airlines maintenance facility." This is when God first began to speak to me. I thought my mind was playing tricks on me because I had never heard of ASA (Atlantic Southeast Airlines) having a maintenance facility and I hadn't ever heard God speak to me in an audible voice before. I decided to be obedient to the spirit of God and when I got home I began to search the yellow pages for the number. I found the number, called out there and was told that they were taking applications for a job in the parts department and to come out the next day and pick up one. I did just that and was later called in for an interview.

As I walked into the room of applicants to be interviewed, I looked around the room and noticed that I was the only female and the only black out of about 15 applicants. For some odd reason, I wasn't surprised. God began to bring to my remembrance the advantage of being different. During the interview process, I was asked where I had gotten the number from to call for an application. I responded by saying, the yellow pages. My soon to be boss (I had learned to speak those things as thou they are) informed me that the number was not listed in the yellow pages. I immediately knew it was God. I would later learn in life that God always provides the resources for his children to get to where he is directing them. I was hired with a salary of what I had asked God for, a salary that equals the two jobs I was working. I was beginning to experience the favor of God. **Halleluiah praise God.**

The job was different from anything that I had ever experienced but I liked it. My supervisor was a great individual and took the time to train me. After several weeks of training, I began working a four day ten hour night shift. I knew this would take much discipline and I was prepared to do just that. God was at work once again teaching me how to become a disciplined individual. A lesson that I would learn later in life would be greatly needed for the task that God had in store for me.

I knew God had blessed me with this job and that he would never send me to a place without already having made the provisions. I would soon learn that the things that God had taught me up to this point was about to be exercised. God had placed me in a place where my faith would be tested.

As I settled into my new job role, I met many new faces. Everyone seemed so laid back and relaxed and the job was easy.

One cold rainy night there was an unscheduled aircraft that came into the facility and needed some major repairs. This caused the maintenance supervisor to develop an attitude with everyone around him. He was known for his ungodly actions but he and I had gotten alone fine until this particular night. He wanted me to locate a part (without giving me the complete description of it) that I couldn't find and he blew up at me. This was the start of many mishaps with him. At this time in my life, God was teaching me that people are people and nothing more; but God is God and nothing less. I continued to trust God because I knew **"No weapon that is formed against thee shall prosper; and every tongue that shall rise against thee in judgment thou shalt condemn. This is the heritage of the servants of the LORD, and their righteousness is of me, saith the Lord" (ISAIAH 54:17).**

One and a half years later, I grew tired of having to work on my off days, different shifts, going in and out of the weather, and having to deal with the different personalities so I began to put in applications all over town, even McDonalds, but there was no job for me. I thought to myself, "This is so strange that I can't even get a job at McDonalds," but God had another plan for me. God was teaching me how to be patient while in a storm, to never give up, don't quit, to be content in my present situation because the best is yet to come. You see, God blocked what I wanted so I would get to what he wanted for me.

Weeks turned into months and months turned into years but one day a job in the front office came open where I would be able to work Monday thru Friday, 8-5p.m. I applied for the job and was given it. I was once again able to become active in the church. I would later in life look back and recognize the fact that God was using this job to walk me into the destiny that he had planned for my life. I could hear God saying, **"For I know the thoughts that I think toward you, saith the LORD, thoughts of peace, and not of evil, to give you an expected end" (JEREMIAH 29:11).**

The more I worked in Gods house, the more revelation he gave me. I began to have a passion for the word of God like never before. I knew he was doing something in my life but I didn't know what. I began to hear God ministering to my heart, and talking to me audibly but I didn't want anyone to think I was crazy so I kept quite. One night during mission, the teacher introduced the book of Jabez. For some reason this book stuck out. I went and purchased it. I began to spend my lunch hour at the park on a daily basis, reading this book; I began to say the Jabez prayer daily. The teacher had shared with us about the power of saying it for 40 days consistently. As I began to say it, things began to take place in my life. God continued to speak to me. At times it was almost as if he was sitting in front of me having a conversation. I felt a love that I had never experienced before.

I remember one particular day as I was sitting in the park, reading the book of Jabez. I heard the Lord call my name. At first I thought someone was in the park that knew me so I began to look around. As I looked, I noticed that the park was empty except for me. I then began to think I was hearing things but then he said it again. As I looked up, I saw the trees above me blowing as if they were waving to get my attention. I then recognized that this was God talking to me and I began to talk to him because I felt so protected.

Later in life, I would discover that when God is all you have God is all you need.

I continued going to the park daily in high hopes of talking to God. I looked forward to our meetings. This became a place of peace and serenity for me. Later in life I would discover that this is the place (parks) I ran to when I was hurting and needed to feel the presence of God.

CHAPTER 4

STORMS OF LIFE

It seems that the closer I tried to get to God, the more storms raged in my life. Here the devil was again at work trying to distract me from where God was leading me. He knew that I was too caught up for the moment to use me, so he took a shot at me through my son.

My son began to experience different things in life and veered towards negative surroundings. He began to abuse his body with drugs and alcohol. He became very disrespectful and uncontrollable. I began to cry out to the Lord to please save my child. I continued to press forward trusting God every step of the way. There were times I bent way down but I did not break. I had decided that I may fall down, but I would get back up again. I pictured myself as a tree planted by the waters growing day by day. I knew who I was and whose I was. I continued studying the word of God. I knew I was treading deep waters and I had to be sure that in times of trouble my anchor would hold. I knew that reading Gods word was not enough, that I had to have it in my heart also, so when the devil caught me without my ammo that I would still know what thus saith the Lord. I was learning that if God bring you to it, he will bring you through it. By now the devil was becoming furious because I was still calling upon the name of the Lord to help me through. Once again he began to stir up things in my marriage. Julius began to take the frustrations that he had against me out on my son. This eventually led to Julius and my son coming up against each other and my son moving out. Oh how my heart ached. I did the only thing I knew to do which was to cry out to the Lord.

The devil was probably thinking, "I've moved in her family, marriage, and child, and she is still calling upon the name of the Lord, what can I do next?" He began to tackle my body. I was diagnosed with ovarian cancer. When I first received the news I was alone, at least I thought I was alone. I tried to reach different family members by phone, but no one could be reached. I began to cry out to the Lord. As I cried, a calmness came over me and I knew I wasn't alone. I realized that God had placed me in a position so I could lean solely upon him and know that no matter how many people I thought could help me that he was the only one who could.

The doctor told me I needed surgery immediately. Surgery had always been one of my greatest fears. I would later recognize that this was Gods plan to get me to another level. I realized that God was allowing me to go through this to build patience, character, humbleness, and faith. Because I loved God and trusted him at his word, before agreeing to a date for surgery, I went before the church for prayer. I remembered the scripture **"Is any sick among you? let him call for the elders of the church; and let them pray over him, anointing him with oil in the name of the LORD" (James 5:14).**

I knew I had to stand on Gods word totally. I didn't know if God would heal me, but I knew he could if he wanted to. The following Tuesday I went for a final test and was told that the cancer was still visible. At this point I didn't understand why and where God was taking me but I knew he held my future and either way I was coming out a winner. The date for my surgery was set for that Friday. I continued to pray but at this point for peace about my destiny. God gave me that peace just before I went into surgery. You see we serve an on time God. He sends us what we need when we need it.

When the doctors went into surgery they expected to remove parts of other organs surrounding the cancer and implant a device where chemo could be administered through but God had another plan. There was no cancer visible. God had healed my body. You see temporary setbacks create opportunities for fresh commitment and renewal. There were many challenging days ahead but my mother was there to help me along the way. I had to undergo many difficult days but God was still in the plan. Many days I lay in the bed reading, praying, and crying. I believed there was a brighter day in my future. I promised the Lord that I would serve him all the days of my life. Whenever you see me acting out of the ordinary for God, it's because I have a reason. God has been too good to me for me to turn around now. You see what the devil meant for evil, God turned to good. Through all the trials and tribulations that I encountered, I gained strength. After the rain and storm, the sun did shine. I realized that God was shaping me by teaching me how to have faith and trust him in all things, for he tells me in his word, **"In all thy ways acknowledge him, and he shall direct thy paths" (Proverbs 3:6).**

You got to know that even when the circumstances make a situation look bleak, that if God chooses not to deliver you in the way you expect, you're still in good hands. I had no idea what was going to take place next, but I knew that God had everything under control.

During my period of recovery, I continued to study Gods word and seek him for guidance. I began to miss the fellowship of the saints and was anxiously awaiting the time when I could join them in the house of the Lord. I began to feel as if God had a special calling upon my life but I didn't want others to think I was crazy, so I kept quite and tried to dismiss the thought that was going through my mind. I continued to study. The more I learned, the more excited I became and wanted to learn. By now I had truly caught on to what being a child of God was all about. I began to put on the whole armor of God, for I knew I was in for a dirty fight with the devil. I was bound and determined to praise God no matter what was placed in my path. I knew that the devils motive was to distract me from where God was leading me. He tried to magnify the problems that were taking place but I knew nothing was bigger than God. I developed a daily prayer life with a prayer partner. I saw God move in the lives of many. God was shaping me by teaching me that mans extremities are his opportunities.

As my body continued to heal physically, I returned to the house of God. I didn't realize where God was taking me but I knew he had a mighty work for me. I continued to work in different areas of the church and trust God. It felt so good to once again be able to fellowship with other believers.

I looked good on the outside but inside I felt like I was being ripped apart. My marriage was at its worse, my son was still roaming the streets, and my grandmother was in her final stages of her life here on earth. The devil probably figured I would break, but I had too much faith to give him the victory over my life for **PHILIPPIANS 4:13** says, **"I can do all things through Christ which strengthened me."**

I continued to pray because I knew much prayer, much power. I had learned that storms of life came to make me stronger, to purify me of all the impurities that were within me so when God began to restore me with the blessings that he has for me, I would be ready to receive them.

Even as I worked diligently within the church, still, the storms kept raging.

Many of times I had heard my mother say, "When your children get off your lap, they will get on your heart." I didn't really understand what she was saying until it happened to me. My son was still roaming from place to place, doing whatever he thought was necessary to survive. If you've ever had a child that the devil had a hold of, you know what I'm feeling. My heart ached so badly and I felt caught in a web, not knowing what to do except pray. Many of times, I saw him walking around town in the cold rainy weather with no place to go. Julius didn't understand that a mother's heart looks at what you can become and not what you appear to be at the present moment. He acted like I shouldn't care because of the chances my son had been given to change. My mind said, leave him alone and let him grow up but my heart said, try again. At this present time in my life I didn't know it but God was teaching me how to be compassionate and to love in spite of. As I pressed on, I was faced with the reality that my life was changing before my eyes and there was nothing I could do about it.

As I continued through my daily activities, I kept seeking God for guidance. God gave me grace.

CHAPTER 5

LOVE ALIVE MINISTRY

God allowed his spirit of revelation to enter the heart of a Christian lady in the church about a ministry for young ladies. After my pastor agreed, a time and date was set for all ladies to come together. None of us knew where this would lead up to but God did. He had already preordained this ministry, the name it was to be, and who would be over it. During this meeting, officers were to be elected, and it was to be given a name. I only wanted to work in the ministry, not be an officer, so I didn't attend the meeting. God had other plans. I was elected president in my absence. When I found out, I quickly declined. The spirit of God was so heavy upon a certain woman of God that I was to be the president that she became persistence by asking my brother, (who at that time didn't believe in women in leadership positions), to talk to me about accepting the role as president of the ministry. He came to me and tried to convince me. I knew this had to be God.

God wouldn't allow me to rest about my decision so I finally agreed. My first thought was, "I have no idea how to be a president," you see, I had taken my focus off of God and started thinking it was about me. God began to minister to me. He allowed me to know that he would never send me to do a job that I was not prepared to do. He said to me that if I would just trust him, that he would direct my path. I began to open up my mind to listen to what God had to say to me. God began a mighty work through me in this ministry. He began to feed me so many things to do within the ministry that I soon forgot about all the problems that I thought I had. I began to exercise all the gifts that God had empowered inside of me. All of the shaping that he had done in me from birth to now, I was about to see come alive. You see, God had taken me through many valley experiences so when he allowed me to have a mountain top experience that I would know how to handle it. Through all of the years of shaping that God had done in me, I had learned how to be humble, compassionate, and to love unconditionally. I had learned how to cry but continue in the work that God had for me to do. I had learned that I must continue on the road if I had to go by myself.

As I continued working in the Love Alive ministry I developed a relationship with the young ladies. A relationship that became bonded through the many trials and tribulations that each of us experienced. We learned how to love each other unconditionally and love God even more. We discovered how to open up our lives enough for others to see that we too cried, laughed, and hurt. Together, through God, we overcame many obstacles in our lives.

The pressures of everyday life were weighing heavily upon me but still I pressed on.

It was at this time in my life that God placed in my spirit that, "When you are experiencing your greatest failures in life, is when you are getting ready to experience your greatest blessing."

God was teaching me the lesson of rising above the circumstances and not allowing the circumstances to rise over me.

After many attempts to save my marriage, I moved out. My oldest daughter decided to stay with her daddy so my younger daughter and I moved into an apartment some 20 miles away. My heart ached so much. I felt shallow, like my heart had been taken out of my body and pounced on. I was a walking Zombie just wandering around in a land of the unknown. Because I loved God so much, I continued in his work.

I trusted him to direct my paths. As I look back, I realized that my darkest hours were the most powerful times in my life. God used me mightily during those times. He opened up my mind and gave me the instructions of how to lead the ministry that he had placed me over. He gave me the strength to accept the things I couldn't change and power to change the things I could. I came to know God as my comforter. The more I read and studied God's word the more revelation he gave me. I became more enlighten of my purpose on earth and engulfed myself into God's work and God's people. We became a family that shared the good times as well as the bad times together. I felt so much love but yet so empty.

During this transition in my life, I had much support from my family as well as my Love Alive family.

The ladies within the ministry gathered around me, prayed for me, and encouraged me to continue on the path that God had ordained for me.

After a while, life began to take a turn for the better and I praised God for it. I began to see the results of the labor that God had entrusted through me. The young ladies were beginning to seek God for direction and love each other unconditionally. There were many supportive sponsors of this ministry that encouraged us to keep on striving to be God's best. (My mother was one of those sponsors who constantly prayed for me. She encouraged me to continue in the fight and to be all that God had called me to be).

They never talked down to any of us, only loved us. There kindness will never be forgotten.

The more God gave me, the more I gave to the ministry. I began to speak things into existence without knowing it at that time. I often made the statement "God has a mighty work for me and that he was going to move me to an unfamiliar territory, around unfamiliar people, to do an extraordinary work." I had no idea at that time how true that statement would later become.

In the mist of all this, God was still at work shaping me for yet an even higher calling.

God began to awake me up in the middle of the night and give me assignments to enhance the growth of the Love Alive ministry. Some of the tasks given were unbelievable but I continued to follow God's instructions. Sometimes I said to God, "Those people are going to think I am crazy". God said to me, "you just do what I have told you to do," so I continued taking the ideals that God had given me to the ministry. Every time I presented an idea that God had given me; there was always someone within the ministry that God had given the knowledge of completing the task. **God got it like that**. He will set you up to bless you up.

The ministry began to grow in leaps and bounds spiritually, physically, emotionally and financially. There were young ladies coming from areas all around our city to be apart of the ministry. God was moving. He was showing each of us his power.

At this time in my life I was learning to just trust God even if it didn't make sense and to know that he has already paved the way for whatever tasks he gives you to do.

God prepared the hearts of the women in the Love Alive Ministry to follow leadership. I thank God for that.

I will forever be grateful for those special women of God that served diligently in the Love Alive Ministry.

CHAPTER 6

BECOMING A MATURE CHRISTIAN

Beginning life as a single parent was scary. Money was scarce, car repairs were needed, and I had no emotional support from a partner. During this time I could have lost my mind but I had an anchor with God that surpasses all understanding of the natural eye. As I went through these distressing times, I remembered God's word, **"The LORD shall preserve thee from all evil: he shall preserve thy soul. The LORD shall preserve thy going out and thy coming in from this time forth, and even for evermore" (Psalm 121:7-8).**

God revealed to me that even though the road was rocky that he would always be there to help me along the way.

Yes, I had to give up some things but I was bound and determined to make it. God had built a fire within me that I didn't understand but I knew he had my back so I pressed on.

As I began to cry out to God about all the circumstances I was facing, he told me to do all I can and wait for him to do the rest. God was teaching me what faith really was. For his word says, **"Now faith is the substance of things hoped for, the evidence of things not seen" (Hebrews 11:1).**

At this time in my life, I can truly say that hope kept me alive. God ordered my steps and I followed.

I applied for a second job at a nearby McDonalds to supplement my income. By now I had learned from God through his word to ask for what I wanted for his word says, **"If ye abide in me, and my words abide in you, ye shall ask what ye will, and it shall be done unto you" (John 15:7).**

I knew I wanted to be off on Mondays, Wednesdays, and Sundays so I would be available for the different ministry fellowships and services, so I requested those days off. I was blessed with the job and the days off I had asked for. I was so thankful that I knew God's word and exercised it. This was a great task for me because I worked for the airline during the day and worked nights at McDonalds. I hardly had enough time to go home and change but I made it.

I continued working at McDonalds, (the same job I had applied for years earlier and could not get).

God does have a sense of humor. He has a path set for each of us and it will be done in his time, not ours.

I meet many people coming and going through those doors that I witnessed to about God's goodness. Some were homeless and their spirits were wreaked. I realized that God had placed me there to condition and shape me even more. As I ministered to the people, their perseverance was a ministry to me. They faced many challenges that I could only identify with through the television land. Praise God for his goodness and mercy.

As I continued working, witnessing and waiting on God to move me in the direction he had for me, I learned how to become satisfied. God was teaching me endurance, patience, and humility. Sometimes that's a hard place to be. I began to see God's creations and his art work. The things that I had never stopped long enough to notice before.

I could hear God speaking to me through the clouds, the trees, and even the birds had a word. I began to see the majesty of God.

In the coming months there was an ice storm that caused the entire town to be without electricity, my grandmother died, and my oldest daughter wasn't talking to me. I did the only thing I knew to do, **"SEEK GOD"**.

I made it by praising my way through. I kept reading and studying God's word, and seeking his divine wisdom for my life. I begin to feel a longing for a place that I knew nothing of. I couldn't understand what I was feeling but I knew it had to be God.

As time went on God would reveal to me what my next steps would be.

God was about to move me to that unfamiliar place that I had previously unknowingly prophesied to myself.

The airline I was working for announced that they were re-locating and I had an option to move with the company and keep my job. Since I was the sole provider and had no other income, I didn't have a choice but to move. You see, I was learning that when God say move, you got to move. He will use any means necessary to get you to where he has for you to be. God will place you in a position where you have no choice but to obey. God used my employer to move me to the place he had chosen for me to be. You see, God knew that I would never do it on my own because I was too attached to my familiar surroundings so he placed me in a position where I had no choice in the matter. Now I understood why God would not allow me to leave that job earlier.

After the initial shock wore off I knew what I had to do. I realized that this was God's way of putting me where he could have my full attention and continue a mighty work through me.

I was happy but yet sad because I had to leave behind two families (my immediate family and the Love Alive family). I didn't know how life in another city would turn out, especially since I had never lived that far away from home, but I knew and trusted that God had made the provisions.

I didn't know it then but God was using my leadership in the Love Alive Ministry as a stepping stone to move me further into the destiny that he had designed for my life. What a mighty God we serve.

On March 1, 2003, I relocated to Arlington, Texas. My entire family agreed to help in the transition. I was so thankful for them.

After settling into my apartment, God instantly begin shaping me. I was in a position where I continued learning perseverance, patience, and how to become satisfied in a storm. I was faced with many obstacles that I had to overcome.

I had to learn a new city, become familiar with my new job duties, develop a relationship with my new co-workers, adjust to living with a room mate, and find a new church home. I knew the most important thing was finding a new church family. As I prayed, God lead me to the place he had already prepared for me to be. Later in life, God would reveal to me that I was placed at that particular church so that he could develop me. You see, God chooses our church home, not us. That is why it is so important to obey God and his choices for our lives. Our church home is where God sends his messages to us through the shepherd that he has placed over us. We must always respect the shepherd and the place where God sends us so that we can get all that he has for us. God had placed me where he wanted me to be so that he could develop me to the point of who he wanted me to become.

Little did I know; there were many storms headed my way, but God knew. He was preparing me for it by allowing me to develop a higher praise for him. He knew that the only way for survival without losing my mind would be to shout my way through it.

At this time in my life, God was teaching me how to praise my way through a storm for when praises go up, blessings come down.

My living conditions were not as I had expected them to be, my children were having some problems, my estranged husband contested the divorce, and my health was beginning to plunge. I couldn't understand why God would move me from my family and then allow me to go through so much pain. God was shaping me by teaching me that when God is all you have, God is all you need.

I had begun to have pains in my left breast and sought out a doctor in the area. After numerous tests my results were sent to a breast specialist. I began to cry out to God. I said, "You brought me here, I am away from my family, depressed, sick, and I may have to be off from work for a lengthy time, what am I suppose to do"? God said to me, **"Get up and praise me, for I am the same God that I was before I allowed these problems to come into your life, trust me and don't doubt me, know that whatever the outcome of your situation is that I am still God and all I have to do is speak the word to your situation."**

I began to prepare to die for I realized that dying is living. I had to die to the thinking and acting like the world in order to live like the word.

I called the doctor to set up an appointment and then I called my mother to tell her the news. She told me she would come and be with me.

The day of my appointment had arrived and my mother, my daughter and I were sitting in the waiting room. As I look back over my life, I realize that I have been in the waiting room numerous of times in my life. **"I waited patiently for the LORD; and he inclined unto me,**

and heard my cry. He brought me up also out of a horrible pit, out of the miry clay, and set my feet upon a rock, and established my goings. And he hath put a new song in my mouth, even praise unto our God: many shall see it, and fear, and shall trust in the LORD" **(Psalm 40:1-3).**

I would later learn in life that being in the waiting room is not always a bad thing if you are waiting for the right messenger.

As I looked around the room, I saw patients that looked like they had been through chemotherapy and I began to get scared. As I look back at this now I realize that this was the devils way of trying to stop me from walking into the destiny that God had prepared for me. The devil wanted me to die. He knew what God had for me.

My name was called and I alone went back into the examination room. As I walked into the room, I looked up to see my x-rays on the lighted screen. My knees began to buckle as I focused in on the views. The doctor walked in and began to explain to me what she thought she saw. Again I say, what she thought she saw. She asked if there was anyone there with me to comfort me and I said yes. She asked if she could bring them in and I said, "Yes, but first take down the x-rays," I didn't want my family to walk in and see what the doctor thought was there. She agreed to that, and I told her I needed to go the bathroom.

I went into the bathroom and fell down on my knees. I began to cry out to God. I said **"GOD, IT DONT LOOK GOOD BUT I KNOW**

THAT ALL YOU HAVE TO DO IS SPEAK THE WORD AND IT WILL BE GONE." You see, I had come too far and fought too hard to get here and die. I knew God had a special purpose for me and that I would do it.

After getting up and refreshing myself, I walked back into the examination room where my mother and daughter were waiting for me with the doctor. The doctor began to tell of the tests required so she would know what treatments were needed. I agreed to the biopsy so that I could move on to the next level where God was taking me. I was beginning to recognize that with each new level, comes a new devil.

This day I will never forget, but I will also never forget "that this is the day that the Lord has made and I will rejoice and be glad in it."

After leaving the doctor's office, I remember having mixed emotions. Some sad, some angry, and then thankful that I had the right mindset to go the doctor. I tried to figure out how this could be happening to me but then God quickly reminded me that he was God and he had this. You see, the devil was trying to get me to doubt God. This was yet another lesson, I had to learn.

The day the test results were to be revealed, I decided that we wouldn't sit by the phone waiting, but would go shopping. I had placed the circumstance in the hands of the Lord and no matter what, he had it. I realized that there was no sense in me worrying about something that only God could change. Before my mother, daughter and I left out the door, the phone rang and the doctor said that my biopsy was negative. Oh how we praised the Lord.

The devil said I was a goner but God said, "Not yet."

As I began working in my new church home, God began to use me in a different capacity. I was appointed by my pastor to be an assistant teacher. This definitely was a change. The only people I had taught were the children. God was using my pastor to push me into the next realm that he had already prepared for me.

As time went by, I began to get comfortable until one day I received a call from the teacher stating she would not be there and she needed me to teach. My first reaction was fear but then I began to pray and ask God for guidance. As I taught, I felt God's hand upon me, empowering me with the Holy Spirit. Later in life, God would reveal to me that he tries us so that we can see who we are inside.

I soon found out that the teacher would be out for some time due to medical reasons.

I knew I could not do it on my own but I knew that God's greatness is fertilized by human weakness so I surrendered all my doubts, fears and inabilities unto him.

I began to teach the women's mission and began to feel the anointing of God upon my life. My whole being was beginning to change. I developed a passion to teach God's word to God's people.

God began to speak more audibly to me. He would wake me up during the night hours and talk to me. He began to give me visions as well as scriptures to teach on. Strange things began to take place within me. I knew God was prepping me but I wasn't sure what for.

After years of teaching I began to become more comfortable in my present state. It seemed that the ball was in my court. Life was great. As days went by, I once again began to have a longing feeling. I didn't understand what was taking place since all was well. I began to tell my friend girl that I believe that God was getting ready to move me. Now, I didn't really want to move, but I knew something was about to take place. I felt within my spirit that God was calling me to preach his word but I subdued the feeling because I was raised in a small town Baptist church that believed that women didn't preach. Later in life, God would reveal to me that he was God all by himself and he will use whomever he chooses to regardless of gender.

I kept teaching bible study; following God's instructions, but yet scared to walk into another realm for fear I was mistaken. I began to get invitations for speaking engagements at different churches. I continuously grew in God's word.

Little did I know but God was at work once again preparing me for the next chapter of my life. Within the next several months my life would change drastically.

My job announced that they were re-locating to Atlanta, Georgia. My first reaction was fear. I was afraid of being unemployed, afraid of what my future would become, and afraid of change. I immediately called my mother. She told me to just pray and that everything would be alright. I would soon learn that my future didn't belong to me anyhow, but to God. I was made and designed for his purpose and his purpose only.

As I began to pray, I was lead toward going to Atlanta, Georgia but then self got in the way and I began to think about what I wanted. I wanted to be close to my family, I wanted to continue to teach in my church, and I wanted to stay amongst the friends I had.

As time neared for my job to re-locate, I continued to pray and was swayed back and forth, (from what God was saying to what I wanted to do). I would later learn that I was kicking against my destiny that God had prepared for me.

The more I prayed the more God revealed to me what was to be. I prayed and I cried, and I cried and I prayed and I cried. Still God did not change his mind. I couldn't believe that God was getting ready to uproot me once again from my familiar surroundings to an unfamiliar place around unfamiliar people. This was a place that I knew no one and did not know my way around. I had only been to Georgia twice in my life and the last time was one of the worst experiences I had ever endured in a city. I had sworn to never return to Georgia, ever again. Isn't it funny how when you decide not to do something, God will show you something different? I would later in life recognize that the place where I had experienced the greatest fear was the place that God was using for my greatest blessing.

God began to bring back to my remembrance how I once made the statement that **"God was going to move me to an unfamiliar place around unfamiliar people to do an extraordinary work."** As I thought about that statement, I thought that the place was Dallas, the place where I had first re-located. Little did I know that Dallas was only a stepping stone. It was a place where my clay pot was beginning to be shaped but not cured.

I remember many days walking through the airport and seeing the phrase "Ordinary people, Extraordinary places." I would just smile and say to myself, "God is amazing." I took it as a sign of being in the right place at the right time.

As the days moved along my co-workers and I had to make the decision to go or stay. I knew what I needed to do but I decided to do what I wanted to do. I signed my letter of separation from the company.

Afterwards, I went back to my office somewhat pleased about my decision but somewhat disappointed. I once again began to have a longing feeling. This was a feeling that I could not explain or shake.

My boss from Georgia called me and told me he had my separation papers on his desk. He stated that he wasn't going to turn them in because he needed me to come to Georgia and run the Atlanta office. I told him I was sorry but I had decided to stay in the DFW area and find employment there, but God had another plan. God began to wake me up in the night and speak to me about going to Atlanta, Georgia. I told the Lord that I didn't want to go because I didn't know anyone in the city and that I had never been that far away from home to live. I told God that I was afraid to take that step. God reminded me of his word, **"For God hath not given us the spirit of fear; but of power, and of love, and of a sound mind." (II Timothy 1:7)**

God was about to show me that it wasn't what I wanted but what he wanted for me.

I remember calling my brother, Joe, the minister, and asking him what he thought. I expressed to him how God was waking me up and talking to me. He replied, "Well baby girl, you remember Jonah?"

Since this wasn't the answer I was seeking, I asked my mother and I received the same answer. I thought, "This has to be a conspiracy against me." Nobody was giving me the answer I was seeking.

After trying to bargain with God and many sleepless nights, I called my boss and said I would come. He told me he still had my papers on his desk (that he hadn't turned them in to H.R.) because he felt that I would change my mind. God was using my boss to get me to the place he had for me to be.

God was teaching me that when he has something for you to do he will use the necessary folk to get it done.

As I accepted the move of God, I began to get excited about the new chapter in my life.

CHAPTER 7

WALKING IN THE LIGHT

After settling into my apartment, I tried to prepare myself emotionally for the new possibilities that I was about to face. I had no idea what was next but God did.

Several weeks went by and I had not attended any type of church service. My soul was beginning to hunger for God's word. I began to question God. I asked God, **"Why would you take me away from a familiar atmosphere where I was teaching your word, a place that**

I was prospering in, to a place where I know no one and have no church home?"

I could not understand God's reasoning for this. I was angry. As time would go by I would understand that God has a set time for everything.

God did not say a word. He allowed me to pout. (Sometimes God will leave us alone until we recognize that he is in charge, all by himself). I cried a many days and nights until finally I decided to get up and venture out in the city. God was teaching me a valuable lesson. He allowed me to know that even though I have faith, I still got to walk into my blessing. I got to trust him and know that if he sends me, that he has already made the provisions.

As I was driving and talking to God, I asked him for a church home. He directed me onto an unfamiliar road where I noticed a billboard with a nice looking man on it. As I kept driving I thought to myself, that was a good looking man. I kept talking to God asking for a church home when I ran into another billboard with the same man on it. This time the billboard seemed to become magnified. As I looked a little closer, I noticed that this wasn't just a man on the billboard but a pastor of a church and the church's name was on the billboard.

God would later reveal to me that he had already given me what I was asking him for but I was too busy drowning myself in self pity to notice.

As I continued driving down this unfamiliar road, I decided that I would search for the church so that I could attend.

The church looked like an office building on the outside but was huge on the inside. God was at work once again teaching me that things are not always what they appear to be on the outside. He was showing me that as his child, I have to look beyond what I can see to the unseen.

The experience was phenomenal. I had never been apart of a service like this before. This was a mega church with a people that had a mega heart for God. I felt such a renewal and afresh.

As time went by, I meet different co-workers that each made a different impact on my life. They were kind to me and showed me around the city. Many invited me to attend church with them.

I remember one particular time that I went to church with a co-worker whose pastor is a prophet. As the service was going on, the pastor of the church begin to prophesy and pointed towards me and said, "Come here." I began to look around because I didn't figure he was talking to me since I didn't know him and he didn't know me. He kept pointing and then he called me out. I was so embarrassed. He began to tell me to run to the back of the church and then run back to the front. I began to trot but then he shouted, "Run!" (You do know that shouting gets your attention). I ran to the back and then back to the front where I just stood there, embarrassed that he had called me out in front of all these people. Later in life, I was to learn that when you are chosen by God, being called out is not a bad thing, for God teaches us through his word that **"Ye are my witnesses, saith the LORD, and my servant whom I have chosen: that ye may know and believe me, and understand that I am he: before me there was no God formed, neither shall there be after me" (Isaiah 43:10).**

He began to prophesy to me while placing his hand onto my forehead. I could feel him pushing my head but I thought to myself, "I am not faking with God and I am not going out like that." No sooner than the thought entered my mind, I was down. I could feel my body stretched out but I could not open my eyes nor get up. As I lay there and sobbed, I could hear him prophesying over me. I could hear the words that sounded so familiar to me, words that I had heard before, from God. Now, I understood why God had isolated me and sent me to Atlanta Georgia. This was a hard pill to swallow, but I did. When I was able to stand, I told God. "I am yours and I will go and do whatever you want me to do."

On that day, April 2005, I accepted the call from God to preach his word.

As I continued attending the church, *"New Birth South Metropolitan Church",* which was pastored by Pastor Andre' Landers, I began to grow mightily in the Lord. Pastor Landers had such an anointing from God on him that you could not sit in service without feeling the presence of God. I saw drug dealers running to the front giving their lives to God, I saw healing and deliverance taking place, and I saw the gift of tongues being exercised. I experienced the full manifestation of God. It was being revealed before my very eyes. I was so overjoyed. I knew God was powerful and I knew he performed miracles even today but I had never seen it in works like I was experiencing now. The more I attended the services at the church, the more anointing I could feel. I became so close to God that I would be driving down the road and look over to the passenger side and began to have a conversation with God as if I could visually see him. I began to cry out to God, asking him to teach me how to fall more in love with him. My spirit grew even hungrier for God. I looked to God for everything, even the smallest of the smallest details. Things didn't have to make sense to me if God told me to do it.

After many months of visiting *New Birth South Metropolitan Church,* I made *New Birth South Metropolitan Church* my new church home, where I announced my calling from God.

I began to walk into the authority that God had given me by teaching and preaching his word. God was opening doors for me that I never had imagined. He gave me sermons and demonstrations along with them that even shocked me.

I attended conferences, workshops, and seminars, learning all I could about God's holy word. The closer I got to God, the closer he got to me. I began to speak things into existence. I took God literally at his word, not wavering backwards nor forwards.

Wednesday night services were just as powerful as Sunday morning services. I began to come home from work on Wednesdays with an urgency to get to church early. It didn't matter what the weather was like, I knew that if I just made it to God's house, I could weather the storm. I knew that God had the power to speak to the storm and it had to cease for his word says, **"He maketh the storm a calm, so that the waves thereof are still" (Psalm 107:29)**

In the midst of it all, God was continually shaping me by teaching me to forgive those who had despitefully misused me.

I thought that I had left all that baggage in Texas, how wrong I was. There were times that I felt an anger arise because of pass obstacles. God was showing me that distance and new location doesn't make the problem go away, only causes your luggage to be overweight, which costs you more. I fasted a many days seeking God for guidance through the forgiving process. He told me that if you want all that I have, give me all that you have. That was the beginning of the end of the unforgiveness that I had in my heart. As I pressed my way God continued opening doors for me.

You see what I thought was a bad thing, (moving to Atlanta, Georgia), turned out to be one of the best things in my life. I met many new faces; people that blessed many in many ways and traveled to places I never thought I would go. I stayed in the finest of the finest hotels and ate the best of the best foods. I lived my life to the fullest, while experiencing the many joys of life.

God was showing me how rich he was. He supplied me abundantly. I looked to him as my provider, physically, emotionally, financially, and most of all spiritually.

As my mindset began to change and I knew that nothing was impossible through God for his word says, **"For as he thinketh in his heart, so is he: Eat and drink, saith he to thee; but his heart is not with thee" (Proverbs 23:7).**

As I continue on the path that God has ordained for me, I say to each of you, trust God with all your heart, mind, and soul. Remember that you are an ordinary individual but God is an extraordinary God. He is your creator and has nothing but good things for you, for his word says, **"Every good gift and every perfect gift is from above, and cometh down from the father of lights, with whom is no variableness, neither shadow of turning" (James 1:17).**

Know that whatever obstacle you are facing, God has the answer. Fall so much in love with God that he can't turn to the left or to the right without you being there.

If you have not done so, submit yourself unto God and know that he cares for you.

Edwards Brothers,Inc!
Thorofare, NJ 08086
06 December, 2010
BA2010340